YOUR KNOWLEDGE HAS VALUE

Bibliographic information published by the German National Library:

The German National Library lists this publication in the National Bibliography; detailed bibliographic data are available on the Internet at http://dnb.dnb.de .

Imprint:

Copyright © 2018 GRIN Verlag
Print and binding: Books on Demand GmbH, Norderstedt Germany
ISBN: 9783668800465

This book at GRIN:

https://www.grin.com/document/419380

Joish Bosco, Fateh Khan

Stock Market Prediction and Efficiency Analysis using Recurrent Neural Network

GRIN Verlag

GRIN - Your knowledge has value

Since its foundation in 1998, GRIN has specialized in publishing academic texts by students, college teachers and other academics as e-book and printed book. The website www.grin.com is an ideal platform for presenting term papers, final papers, scientific essays, dissertations and specialist books.

Visit us on the internet:

http://www.grin.com/

http://www.facebook.com/grincom

http://www.twitter.com/grin_com

STOCK MARKET PREDICTION AND EFFICIENCY ANALYSIS USING RECURRENT NEURAL NETWORK

A PROJECT REPORT

Submitted by

JOISH J BOSCO

FATEH MD KHAN

ABSTRACT

Forecasting stock market prices have always been challenging task for many business analyst and researchers. In fact, stock market price prediction is an interesting area of research for investors. For successful investment, many investors are interested in knowing about the future situation of the market. Effective prediction systems indirectly help traders by providing supportive information such as the future market direction. Data mining techniques are effective for forecasting future by applying various algorithms to data.

This project aims at predicting stock market by using financial news, Analyst opinions and quotes in order to improve quality of output. It proposes a novel method for the prediction of the stock market closing price. Many researchers have contributed in this area of chaotic forecast in their ways. Fundamental and technical analyses are the traditional approaches so far. ANN is another popular way to identify unknown and hidden patterns in data is used for share market prediction.

In this project, we study the problem of stock market forecasting using Recurrent Neural Network (RNN) with Long Short-Term Memory (LSTM). The purpose of this project is to examine the feasibility and performance of LSTM in stock market forecasting. We optimize the LSTM model by testing different configurations, i.e., a multi-layered feed-forward neural network is built by using a combination of data mining. The Neural Network is trained on the stock quotes using the Backpropagation Algorithm which is used to predict share market closing price. The Accuracy of the performance of the neural network is compared using various out of sample performance measures. Modeling techniques and the architecture of the Recurrent Neural Network will also reported in the paper

TABLE OF CONTENTS

LIST OF FIGURES

LIST OF ABBREVIATIONS

ABBREVIATION	EXPANSION
ANN	ARTIFICIAL NEURAL NETWORK
RNN	RECURRENT NEURAL NETWORK
LSTM	LONG SHORT TERM MEMORY

CHAPTER 1

INTRODUCTION

1.1 GENERAL INTRODUCTION

Modeling and Forecasting of the financial market have been an attractive topic to scholars and researchers from various academic fields. The financial market is an abstract concept where financial commodities such as stocks, bonds, and precious metals transactions happen between buyers and sellers. In the present scenario of the financial market world, especially in the stock market, forecasting the trend or the price of stocks using machine learning techniques and artificial neural networks are the most attractive issue to be investigated. As Giles explained, financial forecasting is an instance of signal processing problem which is difficult because of high noise, small sample size, non-stationary, and non-linearity. The noisy characteristics mean the incomplete information gap between past stock trading price and volume with a future price. The stock market is sensitive with the political and macroeconomic environment. However, these two kinds of information are too complex and unstable to gather. The above information that cannot be included in features are considered as noise. The sample size of financial data is determined by real-world transaction records. On one hand, a larger sample size refers a longer period of transaction records; on the other hand, large sample size increases the uncertainty of financial environment during the 2 sample period. In this project, we use stock data instead of daily data in order to reduce the probability of uncertain noise, and relatively increase the sample size within a certain period of time. By non-stationarity, one means that the distribution of stock data is various during time changing. Non-linearity implies that feature correlation of different individual stocks is various. Efficient Market Hypothesis was developed by Burton G. Malkiel in 1991. In Burton's hypothesis, he indicates

1

that predicting or forecasting the financial market is unrealistic, because price changes in the real world are unpredictable. All the changes in prices of the financial market are based on immediate economic events or news. Investors are profit-oriented, their buying or selling decisions are made according to most recent events regardless past analysis or plans. The argument about this Efficient Market Hypothesis has never been ended. So far, there is no strong proof that can verify if the efficient market hypothesis is proper or not. However, as Yaser claims, financial markets are predictable to a certain extent. The past experience of many price changes over a certain period of time in the financial market and the undiscounted serial correlations among vital economic events affecting the future financial market are two main pieces of evidence opposing the Efficient Market Hypothesis. In recent years, machine learning methods have been extensively researched for their potentials in forecasting and prediction of the financial market. Multi-layer feed forward neural networks, SVM, reinforcement learning, relevance vector machines, and recurrent neural networks are the hottest topics of many approaches in financial market prediction field. Among all the machine learning methods, neural networks are well studied and have been successfully used for forecasting and modeling financial market. "Unlike traditional machine learning models, the network learns from the examples by constructing an input-output mapping for the problem at hand. Such an approach brings to mind the study of nonparametric statistical inference; the term "nonparametric" is used here to signify the fact that no prior assumptions are made on a statistical model for the input data", according to Simon. As Francis E.H. Tay and Lijuan Cao explained in their studies, Neural networks are more noise tolerant and more flexible compared with traditional statistical models. By noise tolerance, one means neural networks have the ability to be trained by incomplete and overlapped data. Flexibility refers to that neural networks have the capability to learn dynamic systems through a retraining process using new data patterns. Long short-term memory is a recurrent neural network introduced by Sepp Hochreite and Jurgen Schmidhuber in 1997. LSTM is designed to forecast, predict and classify time series data even long time lags between vital events happened before. LSTMs have been applied to solve several of problems; among those, handwriting Recognition and speech recognition made LSTM famous. LSTM has copious advantages compared with traditional back-propagation neural networks and normal recurrent neural networks. The constant error back propagation inside memory blocks enables in LSTM ability to overcome long time lags in case of problems similar to those discussed above; LSTM can handle noise, distributed representations, and continuous values; LSTM requires no need for parameter fine-tuning, it works well over a broad range of parameters such as learning rate, input gate bias, and output gate bias. The objective of our project can be generalized into two main parts. We examine the feasibility of LSTM in stock market forecasting by testing the model with various configurations.

1.2 PROBLEM STATEMENT

The stock market appears in the news every day. You hear about it every time it reaches a new high or a new low. The rate of investment and business opportunities in the Stock market can increase if an efficient algorithm could be devised to predict the short term price of an individual stock.

Previous methods of stock predictions involve the use of Artificial Neural Networks and Convolution Neural Networks which has an error loss at an average of 20%.

In this report, we will see if there is a possibility of devising a model using Recurrent Neural Network which will predict stock price with a less percentage of error. And if the answer turns to be **YES**, we will also see how reliable and efficient will this model be.

1.3 TECHNOLOGIES

1.3.1 Python

Python was the language of choice for this project. This was an easy decision for the multiple reasons.

1. Python as a language has an enormous community behind it. Any problems that might be encountered can be easily solved with a trip to Stack Overflow. Python is among the most popular languages on the site which makes it very likely there will be a direct answer to any query.

2. Python has an abundance of powerful tools ready for scientific computing. Packages such as Numpy, Pandas, and SciPy are freely available and well documented. Packages such as these can dramatically reduce, and simplify the code needed to write a given program. This makes iteration quick.

3. Python as a language is forgiving and allows for programs that look like pseudo code. This is useful when pseudocode given in academic papers needs to be implemented and tested. Using Python, this step is usually reasonably trivial.

However, Python is not without its flaws. The language is dynamically typed and packages are notorious for Duck Typing. This can be frustrating when a package method returns something that, for example, looks like an array rather than being an actual array. Coupled with the fact that standard Python documentation does not explicitly state the return type of a method, this can lead to a lot of trials and error testing that would not otherwise happen in a strongly typed language. This is an issue that makes learning to use a new Python package or library more difficult than it otherwise could be.

1.3.2 Numpy

Numpy is python modules which provide scientific and higher level mathematical abstractions wrapped in python. In most of the programming languages, we can't use mathematical abstractions such as $f(x)$ as it would affect the semantics and the syntax of the code. But by using Numpy we can exploit such functions in our code.

Numpy's array type augments the Python language with an efficient data structure used for numerical work, e.g., manipulating matrices. Numpy also provides basic numerical routines, such as tools for finding Eigenvectors.

1.3.3 Scikit Learn

Scikit-learn is a free software machine learning library for the Python programming language. It features various classification, regression and clustering algorithms including support vector machine, random forest, gradient boosting, k-means etc. It is mainly designed to interoperate with the Python numerical and scientific libraries **NumPy** and **SciPy**.

Scikit-learn is largely written in Python, with some core algorithms written in **Cython** to achieve performance. Support vector machines are implemented by a Cython wrapper around **LIBSVM** .i.e., logistic regression and linear support vector machines by a similar wrapper around **LIBLINEAR**.

1.3.4 TensorFlow

TensorFlow is an open source software library for numerical computation using data flow graphs. Nodes in the graph represent mathematical operations, while the graph edges represent the multidimensional data arrays (tensors) communicated between them. The flexible architecture allows you to deploy computation to one or more CPUs or GPUs in a desktop, server, or mobile device with a single API. TensorFlow was originally developed by researchers and engineers working on the Google Brain Team within Google's Machine Intelligence research organization for the purposes of conducting machine learning and deep neural networks research, but the system is general enough to be applicable in a wide variety of other domains as well.

TensorFlow is Google Brain's second-generation system. While the reference implementation runs on single devices, TensorFlow can run on multiple CPUs and GPUs (with optional CUDA and SYCL extensions for general-purpose computing on graphics processing units). TensorFlow is available on 64-bit Linux, macOS, Windows, and mobile computing platforms including Android and iOS.

1.3.5 Keras

Keras is a high-level neural networks API, written in Python and capable of running on top of TensorFlow, CNTK, or Theano. It was developed with a focus on enabling fast experimentation. Being able to go from idea to result with the least possible delay is key to doing good research.

Keras allows for easy and fast prototyping (through user friendliness, modularity, and extensibility). Supports both convolutional networks and recurrent networks, as well as combinations of the two. Runs seamlessly on CPU and GPU.

The library contains numerous implementations of commonly used neural network building blocks such as layers, objectives, activation functions, optimizers, and a host of tools to make working with image and text data easier. The code is hosted on GitHub, and community support forums include the GitHub issues page, a Gitter channel and a Slack channel.

1.3.6 Compiler Option

Anaconda is a freemium open source distribution of the Python and R programming languages for large-scale data processing, predictive analytics, and scientific computing, that aims to simplify package management and deployment. Package versions are managed by the package management system conda.

CHAPTER 2

LITERATURE SURVEY

The following papers were studied in order to get an overview of the techniques that were applied earlier to predict the stock market.

LSTM Fully Convolutional Networks for Time Series Classification

-Fazle Karim, Somshubra Majumdar, Houshang Darabi and Shun Chen [1]

With the proposed models, we achieve a potent improvement in the current state-of-the-art for time series classification using deep neural networks. Our baseline models, with and without fine-tuning, are trainable end-to-end with nominal preprocessing and are able to achieve significantly improved performance.

LSTM-FCNs are able to augment FCN models, appreciably increasing their performance with a nominal increase in the number of parameters. An LSTM-FCNs provide one with the ability to visually inspect the decision process of the LSTM RNN and provide a strong baseline on their own. Fine-tuning can be applied as a general procedure to a model to further elevate its performance.

The strong increase in performance in comparison to the FCN models shows that LSTM RNNs can beneficially supplement the performance of FCN modules for time series classification. An overall analysis of the performance of our model is provided and compared to other techniques.

There is further research to be done on understanding why the attention LSTM cell is unsuccessful in matching the performance of the general LSTM cell on some of the datasets. Furthermore, an extension of the proposed models to multivariate time series is elementary but has not been explored in this work.

Learning Long term Dependencies with Gradient Descent is difficult

-Yoshua bengio, Patrice Simard and Paolo Frasconi [10]

Recurrent networks are very powerful in their ability to represent context, often outperforming static network. But the factor off gradient descent of an error criterion may be inadequate to train them for a task involving long-term dependencies. It has been found that the system would not be robust to input noise or would not be efficiently trainable by gradient descent when the long-term context is required. The theoretical result presented in this paper holds for any error criterion and not only from mean square error.

it can also be seen that the gradient either vanishes or the system is not robust to input noise. The other imp factor to note is that the related problems of vanishing gradient may occur in deep feed-forward networks. The result presented in this paper does not mean that it is impossible to train a recurrent neural network on a particular task. It says that the gradient becomes increasingly inefficient when the temporal span of the dependencies increases. So at one point in time, it is evident that it becomes obsolete.

Improving N Calculation of the RSI Financial Indicator Using Neural Networks

-Alejandro Rodríguez-González, Fernando Guldris Iglesias, Ricardo Colomo-Palacios Giner Alor-Hernandez, Ruben Posada-Gomez [8]

There has been growing interest in Trading Decision Support Systems in recent years. In spite of its volatility, it is not entirely random, instead, it is nonlinear and dynamic or highly complicated and volatile. Stock movement is affected by the mixture of two types of factors: determinant (e.g. gradual strength change between buying side and selling side) and random (e.g. emergent affairs or daily operation variations).

There are 3 modules that are talked about in this research paper. The Neural Network Module is responsible for providing the N values that are used to calculate RSI and decide if an investor should invest in a certain company.

Trading system Module analyzes the result given by neural network module. When a query is formulated to the system, it takes the actual values of the market and builds a query to the neural network. If RSI value is higher than 70 the decision that trading system return is a sell signal. If RSI value is lower than 30 the decision that trading system return is a buy signal.

The heuristic module is in charge of managing the different formulas that provide the heuristic used to generate the optimal values for RSI indicator.

Stock Trend Prediction Using Simple Moving Average Supported

by News Classification

-Stefan Lauren Dra. Harlili S., M.Sc. [5]

The simple moving average is one of many time series analysis technique. Time series analysis is a method of timely structured data processing to find statistics or important characteristics for many reasons. The simple moving average shows stock trend by calculating the average value of stock prices on specific duration. The prices that are used are closing prices at the end of the day. This technique can avoid noises and therefore smooth the trend movement.

The main objective of financial news classification is to classify and calculate each news' sentiment value. The positive news is marked by sentiment value which is greater than 0, while negative news is marked by less than 0 sentiment value. If there are news having 0 sentiment value, they will be omitted as their neutralism does not affect the stock trend.

Machine learning using artificial neural network algorithm is used to predict a stock trend. The artificial neural network uses three features along with one label. The three features are a simple moving average distance which is a subtraction of long-term and short-term simple moving average, the total value of positive sentiment value for one-day news, and the total value of negative sentiment value for one-day news. Stock trend label is used and classified as uptrend and downtrend. On one hand, learning component is done by a background process. On the other hand, prediction component is foreground process which is seen and interact with the user.

VISUALIZING AND UNDERSTANDING RECURRENT NETWORKS

-Andrej Karpathy, Justin Johnson, Li Fei-Fei [4]

Character-level language models have been used as an interpretable test bed for analyzing the predictions, representations training dynamics, and error types present in Recurrent Neural Networks. In particular, the qualitative visualization experiments, cell activation statistics and comparisons to finite horizon n-gram models demonstrate that these networks learn powerfully, and often interpretable long-range interactions on real-world data.

The error analysis broke down cross entropy loss into several interpretable categories and allowed us to illuminate the sources of remaining limitations and to suggest further areas for study.

In particular, it was found that scaling up the model almost entirely eliminates errors in the n-gram category, which provides some evidence that further architectural innovations may be needed to address the remaining errors.

LSTM: A Search Space Odyssey

-Klaus Greff, Rupesh K. Srivastava, Jan Koutn'ık, Bas R. Steunebrink, Jurgen Schmidhuber [3]

This paper reports the results of a large-scale study on variants of the LSTM architecture. We conclude that the most commonly used LSTM architecture (vanilla LSTM) performs reasonably well on various datasets. None of the eight investigated modifications significantly improves performance.

The forget gate and the output activation function are the most critical components of the LSTM block. Removing any of them significantly impairs performance. We hypothesize that the output activation function is needed to prevent the unbounded cell state to propagate through the network and destabilize learning. This would explain why the LSTM variant GRU can perform reasonably well without it: its cell state is bounded because of the coupling of input and forget gate.

The analysis of hyperparameter interactions revealed no apparent structure. Furthermore, even the highest measured interaction (between learning rate and network size) is quite small. This implies that for practical purposes the hyperparameters can be treated as approximately independent. In particular, the learning rate can be tuned first using a fairly small network, thus saving a lot of experimentation time.

Neural networks can be tricky to use for many practitioners compared to other methods whose properties are already well understood. This has remained a hurdle for newcomers to the field since a lot of practical choices are based on the intuitions of experts, as well as experiences gained over time. With this study, we have attempted to back some of these intuitions with experimental results. We have also presented new insights, both on architecture selection and hyperparameter tuning for LSTM networks which have emerged as the method of choice for solving complex sequence learning problems. In future work, we plan to explore more complex modifications of the LSTM architecture.

The difficulty of training recurrent neural networks

-Razvan Pascanu, Tomas Mikolov, Yoshua Bengio [6]

We provided different perspectives through which one can gain more insight into the exploding and vanishing gradients issue. We put forward a hypothesis stating that when gradients explode we have a cliff-like structure in the error surface and devise a simple solution based on this hypothesis, clipping the norm of the exploded gradients.

The effectiveness of our proposed solutions provides some indirect empirical evidence towards the validity of our hypothesis, though further investigations are required. In order to deal with the vanishing gradient problem, we use a regularization term that forces the error signal not to vanish as it travels back in time.

This regularization term forces the Jacobian matrices $\partial x_i\, \partial x_i - 1$ to preserve norm only in relevant directions. In practice, we show that these solutions improve the performance of RNNs on the pathological synthetic datasets considered, polyphonic music prediction and language modeling.

Deep Sparse Rectifier Neural Networks

-Xavier Glorot Antoine Bordes Yoshua Bengio [7]

Sparsity and neurons operating mostly in a linear regime can be brought together in more biologically plausible deep neural networks. Rectifier units help to bridge the gap between unsupervised pre-training and no pre-training, which suggests that they may help in finding better minima during training.

This finding has been verified for four image classification datasets of different scales and all this in spite of their inherent problems, such as zeros in the gradient, or ill-conditioning of the parameterization. Rather sparse networks are obtained (from 50 to 80% sparsity for the best generalizing models, whereas the brain is hypothesized to have 95% to 99% sparsity), which may explain some of the benefits of using rectifiers.

Rectifier activation functions have shown to be remarkably adapted to sentiment analysis, a text-based task with a very large degree of data sparsity. This promising result tends to indicate that deep sparse rectifier networks are not only beneficial to image classification tasks and might yield powerful text mining tools in the future.

Furthermore, rectifier activation functions have shown to be remarkably adapted to sentiment analysis, a text-based task with a very large degree of data sparsity. This promising result tends to indicate that deep sparse rectifier networks are not only beneficial to image classification tasks and might yield powerful text mining tools in the future.

Stock Market Trends Prediction after Earning Release

-Chen Qian, Wenjie Zheng [2]

As known to the public, the stock market is known as a chaotic system and it has been proved that even model built with empirical key features could still result in low accuracy. In our work, we tried to limit our scope to earnings release day, and it turned out that we could build models achieving around 70% prediction accuracy.

To build the model, We take financial statistics collected from company's quarterly earnings report, market surprise due to consensus expectations in terms of digital data, and sentiment analysis of relevant articles from mainstream media of financial professionals as two sets of input features, and make stock market movements prediction in after-hour period and trend in the day after the release day. SVM and LWLR model outperforms other models as shown by experiments, as they control the correlation among data, which was discussed in Section VI.

However, due to the limited number of company choices, we have small data size (300 samples) which could lead to high bias and overfitting. The stock price is not only affected by certain financial features, consensus news, but also company direction and future business guidance, which are difficult to be digitized.

Predicting Stock Trends through Technical Analysis and Nearest Neighbor Classification

-Lamartine Almeida Teixeira Adriano Lorena Inácio de Oliveira [9]

Tech Examination is built on the philosophies of the Dow Theory and practices the past of prices to forecast upcoming actions. The method used in tech examination can be enclosed as an outline credit problem, where the ideas are resulting from the history of values and the output is an estimate of the price or an estimate of the prices trend.

 The most significant evidence of this type of examination is that the marketplace action reductions everything. It means the specialist believes that anything that can perhaps affect the marketplace is already reflected in the prices, as well as that all the new evidence will be directly reflected in those prices. As an import, all the technician needs is to analyze the past of prices.

The main gears of the tech examination are the capacity and price charts. Based on the data of values and size the tech pointers are built. Tech pointers are math formulations that are applied to the price or volume statistics of a safekeeping for demonstrating some aspect of the association of those amounts.

CHAPTER 3

DATA AND TOOLS

3.1 Data Used

3.1.1 Choosing the Dataset

For this project, we chose the Google stocks. The Google stocks is a large index traded on the New York stock exchange. All companies in the index are large publicly traded companies, leaders in each of their own sectors. The index covers a diverse set of sectors featuring companies such as Microsoft, Visa, Boeing, and Walt Disney. It is important to use a predefined set of companies rather than a custom selected set so that we do leave ourselves open to methodology errors or accusations of fishing expeditions. If we had selected a custom set of companies, it could be argued that the set was tailored specifically to improve our results. Since the aim of the project is to create a model of stock markets in general. Google was chosen because it is well known. The components provided a good balance between available data and computational feasibility.

3.1.2 Gathering the Datasets

A primary dataset will be used throughout the project. The dataset will contain the daily percentage change in stock price. Luckily, daily stock price data is easy to come by. Google and Yahoo both operate websites which offer a facility to download CSV files containing a full 14 daily price history. These are useful for looking at individual companies but cumbersome when accessing large amounts of data across many stocks. For this reason, Quandl was used to gather the data instead of using Google and Yahoo directly. Quandl is a free to use website that hosts and maintains vast amounts of numerical datasets with a focus specifically on economic datasets, including stock market data which is backed by Google and Yahoo. Quandl also provides a small python library that is useful for accessing the database programmatically. The library provides a simple method for calculating the daily percentage change daily in prices.

For instance, data we gather for a Monday will be matched with, and try to predict, Tuesday's trend. This dataset was then saved in CSV format for simple retrial as needed throughout the project. This dataset containing the daily trends of companies will serve as the core dataset that will be used in most experiments later in the report.

300	3/13/2013	412.4	413.79	409.62	823.05	32,94,800
301	3/14/2013	411.95	411.95	407.17	819.29	33,14,700
302	3/15/2013	407.72	408.62	405.15	812.07	62,22,500
303	3/18/2013	401	404.86	399.24	805.58	36,90,300
304	3/19/2013	404.11	408.1	401.72	809.1	42,12,000
305	3/20/2013	406.89	407.23	404.2	812.48	29,38,500
306	3/21/2013	404.13	406.93	403.41	809.04	29,66,200
307	3/22/2013	405.85	406.1	403.31	808.09	29,87,400
308	3/25/2013	404.69	408.09	401.9	807.42	34,36,800
309	3/26/2013	405.23	405.48	402.39	810.2	23,92,600
310	3/27/2013	401.83	401.99	399.17	800.46	43,42,500
311	3/28/2013	400.49	401.18	395.17	792.02	45,92,600
804	3/13/2015	551.98	556.87	542.73	545.82	17,03,500
805	3/16/2015	549.44	555.33	544.51	552.99	16,40,900
806	3/17/2015	550.2	552.28	546.5	549.33	18,05,500
807	3/18/2015	550.99	558.25	545.5	557.97	21,34,500
808	3/19/2015	557.86	559.26	554.62	556.46	11,97,200
809	3/20/2015	560.11	560.18	557.52	558.83	26,16,800
810	3/23/2015	558.9	560.82	554.31	557.28	16,43,800
811	3/24/2015	561.02	573.02	559.67	568.63	25,83,200
812	3/25/2015	568.94	570.69	557.21	557.26	21,52,200
813	3/26/2015	556.06	557.37	549.14	553.65	15,72,600
814	3/27/2015	551.49	553.76	546.63	546.84	18,97,400
T815	3/30/2015	550.11	551.95	546.67	550.52	12,87,500

Table[4.1]: Dataset

CHAPTER 4

INTEGRATED SUMMARY

The most interesting task is to predict the market. So many methods are used for completing this task. Methods vary from very informal ways to many formal ways a lot. This tech. are categorized as:

- Prediction Methods
- Traditional Time Series
- Technical Analysis Methods
- Machine Learning Methods
- Fundamental Analysis Methods
- Deep Learning

The criteria for this category are the kind of tool and the kind of data that these methods are consuming in order to predict the market. What is mutual to the technique is that they are predicting and hence helping the market's future behavior.

4.1 Technical Analysis Methods

Technical analysis is used to attempt to forecast the price movement of virtually any tradable instrument that is generally subject to forces of supply and demand, including stocks, bonds, futures and currency pairs. In fact, technical analysis can be viewed as simply the study of supply and demand forces as reflected in the market price movements of a security. It is most commonly applied to price changes, but some analysts may additionally track numbers other than just prices, such as trading volume or open interest figures.

Over the years, numerous technical indicators have been developed by analysts in attempts to accurately forecast future price movements. Some indicators are focused primarily on identifying the current market trend, including support and resistance areas, while others are focused on determining the strength of a trend and the likelihood of its continuation. Commonly used technical indicators include trendlines, moving averages and momentum indicators such as the moving average convergence divergence (MACD) indicator.

Technical analysts apply technical indicators to charts of various timeframes. Short-term traders may use charts ranging from one-minute timeframes to hourly or four-hour timeframes, while traders analyzing longer-term price movement scrutinize daily, weekly or monthly charts.

4.2 Fundamental Analysis Techniques

Fundamental analysis uses real, public data in the evaluation a security's value. Although most analysts use fundamental analysis to value stocks, this method of valuation can be used for just about any type of security. For example, an investor can perform fundamental analysis on a bond's value by looking at economic factors such as interest rates and the overall state of the economy. He can also look at information about the bond issuer, such as potential changes in credit ratings.

For stocks and equity instruments, this method uses revenues, earnings, future growth, return on equity, profit margins, and other data to determine a company's underlying value and potential for future growth. In terms of stocks, fundamental analysis focuses on the financial statements of the company being evaluated. One of the most famous and successful fundamental analysts is the so-called "Oracle of Omaha", Warren Buffett, who is well known for successfully employing fundamental analysis to pick securities. His abilities have turned him into a billionaire.

4.3 Traditional Time Series Prediction

Time series analysis can be useful to see how a given asset, security or economic variable changes over time. It can also be used to examine how the changes associated with the chosen data point compare to shifts in other variables over the same time period.

For example, suppose you wanted to analyze a time series of daily closing stock prices for a given stock over a period of one year. You would obtain a list of all the closing prices for the stock from each day for the past year and list them in chronological order. This would be a one-year daily closing price time series for the stock.

Delving a bit deeper, you might be interested to know whether the stock's time series shows any seasonality to determine if it goes through peaks and valleys at regular times each year. The analysis in this area would require taking the observed prices and correlating them to a chosen season. This can include traditional calendar seasons, such as summer and winter, or retail seasons, such as holiday seasons.

Alternatively, you can record a stock's share price changes as it relates to an economic variable, such as the unemployment rate. By correlating the data points with information relating to the selected economic variable, you can observe patterns in situations exhibiting dependency between the data points and the chosen variable.

4.4 Machine Learning Methods

Various sectors of the economy are dealing with huge amounts of data available in different formats from disparate sources. The enormous amount of data, known as Big Data, is becoming easily available and accessible due to the progressive use of technology. Companies and governments realize the huge insights that can be gained from tapping into big data but lack the resources and time required to comb through its wealth of information. In this regard, Artificial Intelligence (AI) measures are being employed by different industries to gather, process, communicate and share useful information from data sets. One method of AI that is increasingly utilized for big data processing is Machine Learning.

The various data applications of machine learning are formed through a complex algorithm or source code built into the machine or computer. This programming code creates a model which identifies the data and builds predictions around the data it identifies. The model uses parameters built into the algorithm to form patterns for its decision-making process. When new or additional data becomes available, the algorithm automatically adjusts the parameters to check for a pattern change, if any. However, the model shouldn't change.

How machine learning works can be better explained by an illustration in the financial world. Traditionally, investment players in the securities market like financial researchers, analysts, asset managers, individual investors scour through a lot of information from different companies around the world to make profitable investment decisions. However, some pertinent information may not be widely publicized by the media and may be privy to only a select few who have the advantage of being employees of the company or residents of the country where the information stems from. In addition, there's only so much information humans can collect and process within a given time frame. This is where machine learning comes in.

An asset management firm may employ machine learning in its investment analysis and research area. Say the asset manager only invests in mining stocks. The model built into the system scans the World Wide Web and collects all types of news events from businesses, industries, cities, and countries, and this information gathered comprises the data set. All the information inputted in the data set is information that the asset managers and researchers of the firm would not have been able to get using all their human powers and intellects. The parameters built alongside the model extracts only data about mining companies, regulatory policies on the exploration sector, and political events in select countries from the data set. Say, a mining company XYZ just discovered a diamond mine in a small town in South Africa, the machine learning app would highlight this as relevant data. The model could then use an analytics tool called predictive analytics to make predictions on whether the mining industry will be profitable for a time period, or which mining stocks are likely to increase in value at a certain time. This information is relayed to the asset manager to analyze and make a decision for his portfolio. The asset manager may make a decision to invest millions of dollars into XYZ stock.

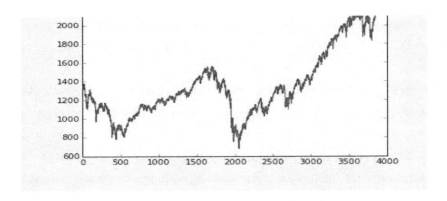

Fig[4.1]: Machine Learning Analysis Curve

In the wake of an unfavorable event, such as South African miners going on strike, the computer algorithm adjusts its parameters automatically to create a new pattern. This way, the computational model built into the machine stays current even with changes in world events and without needing a human to tweak its code to reflect the changes. Because the asset manager received this new data on time, he is able to limit his losses by exiting the stock. Machine learning is used in different sectors for various reasons. Trading systems can be calibrated to identify new investment opportunities. Marketing and e-commerce platforms can be tuned to provide accurate and personalized recommendations to their users based on the users' internet search history or previous transactions. Lending institutions can incorporate machine learning to predict bad loans and build a credit risk model. Information hubs can use machine learning to cover huge amounts of news stories from all corners of the world. Banks can create fraud detection tools from machine learning techniques. The incorporation of machine learning in the digital-savvy era is endless as businesses and governments become more aware of the opportunities that big data presents.

4.5 DEEP LEARNING

An artificial intelligence function that imitates the workings of the human brain in processing data and creating patterns for use in decision making. Deep learning is a subset of machine learning in Artificial Intelligence (AI) that has networks which are capable of learning unsupervised from data that is unstructured or unlabeled. Also known as Deep Neural Learning or Deep Neural Network.

BREAKING DOWN 'Deep Learning'

The digital era has brought about an explosion of data in all forms and from every region of the world. This data, known simply as Big Data, is gotten from sources like social media, internet search engines, e-commerce platforms, online cinemas, etc. This enormous amount of data is readily accessible and can be shared through fine tech applications like cloud computing. However, the data, which normally is unstructured, is so vast that it could take decades for humans to comprehend it and extract relevant information. Companies realize the incredible potential that can result from unraveling this wealth of information and are increasingly adapting to Artificial Intelligence (AI) systems for automated support.

One of the most common AI techniques used for processing Big Data is Machine Learning. Machine learning is a self-adaptive algorithm that gets better and better analysis and patterns with experience or with newly added data. If a digital payments company wanted to detect the occurrence of or potential for fraud in its system, it could employ machine learning tools for this purpose. The computational algorithm built into a computer model will process all transactions happening on the digital platform, find patterns in the data set, and point out any anomaly detected by the pattern.

Deep learning, a subset of machine learning, utilizes a hierarchical level of artificial neural networks to carry out the process of machine learning. The artificial neural networks are built like the human brain, with neuron nodes connected together like a web. While traditional programs build analysis with data in a linear way, the hierarchical function of deep learning systems enables machines to process data with a non-linear approach. A traditional approach to detecting fraud or money laundering might rely on the amount of transaction that ensues, while a deep learning non-linear technique to weeding out a fraudulent transaction would include time, geographic location, IP address, type of retailer, and any other feature that is likely to make up a fraudulent activity. The first layer of the neural network processes a raw data input like the amount of the transaction and passes it on to the next layer as output. The second layer processes the previous layer's information by including additional information like the user's IP address and passes on its result. The next layer takes the second layer's information and includes raw data like geographic location and makes the machine's pattern even better. This continues across all levels of the neuron network until the best and output is determined.

Using the fraud detection system mentioned above with machine learning, we can create a deep learning example. If the machine learning system created a model with parameters built around the amount of dollars a user sends or receives, the deep learning method can start building on the results offered by machine learning. Each layer of its neural network builds on its previous layer with added data like a retailer, sender, user, social media event, credit score, IP address, and a host of other features that may take years to connect together if processed by a human being. Deep learning algorithms are trained to not just create patterns from all transactions, but to also know when a pattern is signaling the need for a fraudulent investigation. The final layer relays a signal to an analyst who may freeze the user's account until all pending investigations are finalized.

Deep learning is used across all industries for a number of different tasks. Commercial apps that use image recognition, open source platforms with consumer recommendation apps, and medical research tools that explore the possibility of reusing drugs for new ailments are a few of the examples of deep learning incorporation.

4.5.1 Artificial Neural Networks (ANN)

A computing system that is designed to simulate the way the human brain analyzes and process information. Artificial Neural Networks (ANN) is the foundation of Artificial Intelligence (AI) and solves problems that would prove impossible or difficult by human or statistical standards. ANN has self-learning capabilities that enable it to produce better results as more data becomes available.

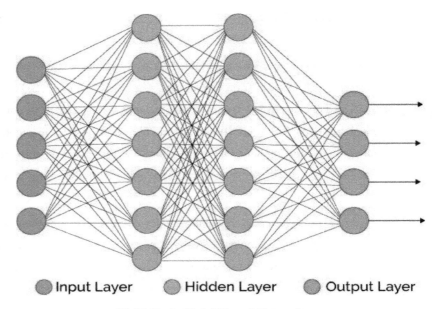

Fig[4.2]: Artificial Neural Network

4.5.1.1 ANN in Stock Market Prediction

It is possible to use Artificial intelligence (AI) to develop models that can be used in prediction. Such models are applicable to the financial markets such as the stock exchange. The AI method that was found suitable for these models was the Artificial Neural Network (ANN), which exploits parallel computing to gain intelligence from input data as a basis for predicting future values. These ANN models, such as the multi-layer perceptron (MLP) using feedforward network with error backpropagation, can be developed into prototypes using typical programming languages such as Python. ANN tools need substantial data for training to enable them to have the capacity of prediction. The research determined that a model of the configuration of 5:21:21:1 achieved an accuracy on an average of 80%. The research also determined that at least 1,000 records, which was 80% of the data, training over 130,000 cycles, was needed for the training set to achieve best results for a prediction of 60 future values (3-

months). Once trained, the ANN-based system was capable of very high precision in its prediction. Validation of the model was done using two open source tools (Encog Workbench and Neuroph).

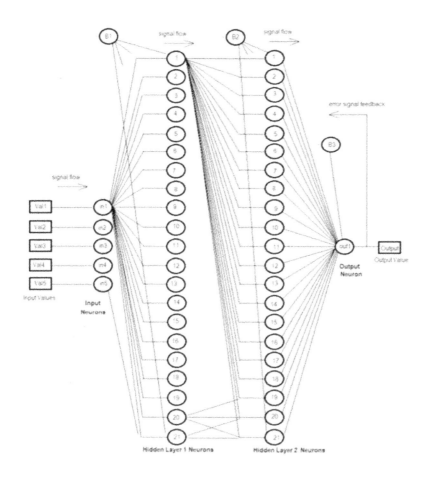

Fig[4.3]: Stock Visualization Curve

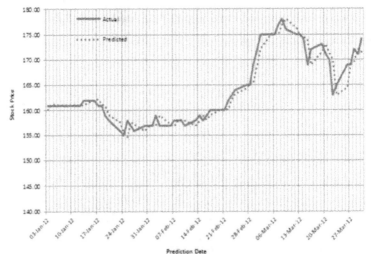

Fig[4.4]: Training Error in ANN

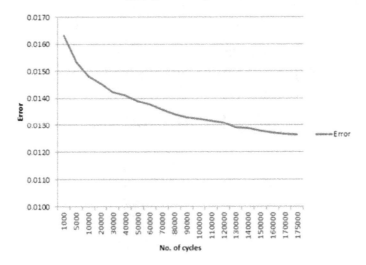

Fig[4.5]: Training ANN based system

4.5.2 CONVOLUTION NEURAL NETWORKS (CNN)

In machine learning, a convolutional neural network is a class of deep, feed-forward artificial neural networks that have successfully been applied to analyzing visual imagery. CNN's use a variation of multilayer perceptrons designed to require minimal preprocessing.They are also known as shift invariant or space invariant artificial neural networks (SIANN), based on their shared-weights architecture and translation invariance characteristics.

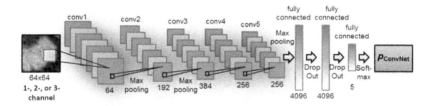

Fig[4.6]: Convolution Neural Networks(CNN)

4.5.2.1 CNN in Stock Market Prediction

For each of the two architectures (the original one, which resulted in blurring of the image by the final layers; and the reduced architecture) and each of the two new types of features, we trained the network, tweaked the hyperparameters until convergence was achieved in at most 10,000 iterations and computed an out–of–sample R2 on a test set of data. The results of that process are shown below

	Original arch.	Reduced arch.
Price windows with volume	−0.05	−0.014
Correlation features	−0.42	−0.013

Table[4.2]:Comparative Results

Overall the results are underwhelming. We were unable to achieve an out–of–sample R2 greater than 0; that is to say, you would be better off guessing that the next price movement is going to be the mean price movement (typically 0) than following our model. Nonetheless, this was a good learning experience.

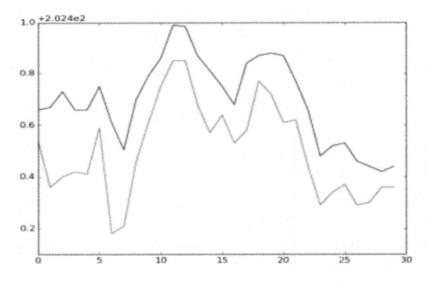

Fig[4.7]: CNN Input Visualization

-High prices are in blue
-Low prices are in green

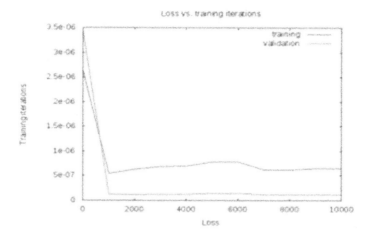

Fig[4.8]: Training and validation loss

CHAPTER 5

OUR PROPOSED MODEL

5.1 RECURRENT NEURAL NETWORK (RNN)

A recurrent neural network (RNN) is a class of artificial neural network where connections between units form a directed cycle. This allows it to exhibit dynamic temporal behavior. Unlike feedforward neural networks, RNNs can use their internal memory to process arbitrary sequences of inputs. This makes them applicable to tasks such as unsegmented, connected handwriting recognition or speech recognition.

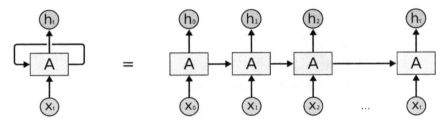

Fig[5.1]: Recurrent Neural Network Architecture

5.2 LONG SHORT TERM MEMORY (LSTM)

Long short-term memory (LSTM) networks were invented by Hochreiter and Schmidhuber in 1997 and set accuracy records in multiple applications domains. Around 2007, LSTM started to revolutionize speech recognition, outperforming traditional models in certain speech applications. In 2009, a Connectionist Temporal Classification (CTC)-trained LSTM network was the first RNN to win pattern recognition contests when it won several competitions in connected handwriting recognition. In 2014, the Chinese search giant Baidu used CTC-trained RNNs to break the Switchboard Hub500 speech recognition benchmark without using any traditional speech processing methods.

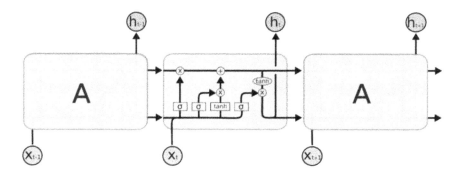

Fig[5.2]: LSTM Architecture

5.3 LSTM

Like most neural networks, recurrent nets are old. By the early 1990s, the vanishing gradient problem emerged as a major obstacle to recurrent net performance.

Just as a straight line expresses a change in x alongside a change in y, the gradient expresses the change in all weights with regard to the change in error. If we can't know the gradient, we can't adjust the weights in a direction that will decrease error, and our network ceases to learn.

For Recurrent networks seeking to establish connections between a final output and events, many time steps before were hobbled, because it is very difficult to know how much importance must be given accord to remote inputs. (Like great-great-grandparents, they multiply quickly in number and their legacy is often obscure.)

This is partly because the information flowing through neural nets passes through many stages of multiplication.

Everyone who has studied compound interest knows that any quantity multiplied frequently by an amount slightly greater than one can become

34

immeasurably large (indeed, that simple mathematical truth underpins network effects and inevitable social inequalities). But its inverse, multiplying by a quantity less than one, is also true. Gamblers go bankrupt fast when they win just 97 cents on every dollar they put in the slots. This is because the layers and time steps of deep neural networks relate to each other through multiplication, derivatives are susceptible to vanishing or exploding.

Exploding gradients treat every weight as though it were the proverbial butterfly whose flapping wings cause a distant hurricane. Those weights' gradients become saturated on the high end; i.e. they are presumed to be too powerful. But exploding gradients can be solved relatively easily because they can be truncated or squashed. Vanishing gradients can become too small for computers to work with or for networks to learn – a harder problem to solve.

Below you see the effects of applying a sigmoid function over and over again. The data is flattened until, for large stretches, it has no detectable slope. This is analogous to a gradient vanishing as it passes through many layers.

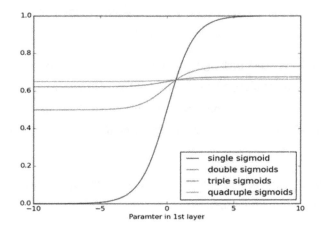

Fig[5.3]: Comparative Sigmoid Curves

5.4 ADVANTAGES OF LSTM.

In the mid-90s, a variation of the recurrent net with so-called Long Short-Term Memory units, or LSTMs, was proposed by the German researchers Sepp Hochreiter and Juergen Schmidhuber as a solution to the vanishing gradient problem.

LSTMs help preserves the error that can be backpropagated through time and layers. By maintaining a more constant error, they allow recurrent nets to continue to learn over many time steps (over 1000), thereby opening a channel to link causes and effects remotely. This is one of the central challenges to machine learning and AI since algorithms are frequently confronted by environments where reward signals are sparse and delayed, such as life itself. (Religious thinkers have tackled this same problem with ideas of karma or divine reward, theorizing invisible and distant consequences to our actions.)

LSTMs contain information outside the normal flow of the recurrent network in a gated cell. Information can be stored in, written to, or read from a cell, much like data in a computer's memory. The cell makes decisions about what to store, and when to allow reads, writes, and erasures, via gates that open and close. Unlike the digital storage on computers, however, these gates are analog, implemented with element-wise multiplication by sigmoids, which are all in the range of 0-1. Analog has the advantage over digital of being differentiable, and therefore suitable for backpropagation.

Those gates act on the signals they receive, and similar to the neural network's nodes, they block or pass on information based on its strength and import, which they filter with their own sets of weights. Those weights, like the weights that modulate input and hidden states, are adjusted via the recurrent networks learning the process. That is, the cells learn when to allow data to enter, leave or be deleted through the iterative process of making guesses, backpropagating error, and adjusting weights via gradient descent.

The diagram below illustrates how data flows through a memory cell and is controlled by its gates.

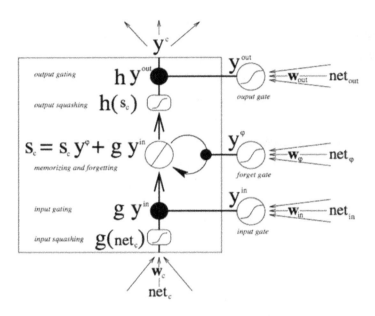

Fig[5.4]: Data flow through the memory cell

CHAPTER 6

SYSTEM DESIGN

6.1 SYSTEM ARCHITECTURE

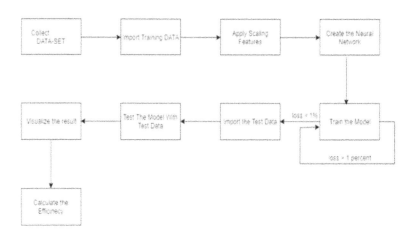

Fig[6.1]: System Architecture

6.1.1 Collect DATA-SET

As discussed before Quandl has been used to collect Google Data-set. This dataset has been stored as a CSV file, which makes it easier for importing and exporting data in python using Pandas library.

6.1.2 Import Training Data

Once the dataset is collected, it has to be split into the training and the test set. Then the training set of data should be imported using the Pandas library and should be made a processable analysis.

6.1.3 Apply Scaling Features

This is one of the most important parts of the process. Once the training data is imported there are possibilities that the values of some are completely out of reference. So it is mandatory to scale the value so that all the values in the data are within a specific range. We will be using the Min-Max Scaler for this process.

6.1.4 Creating a NEURAL NETWORK

Once the data is scaled, the next step is to create an LSTM network. Keras will be used to create this network, and Keras will use Tensorflow at the backend to do it. Keras makes it easier and acts as an API for Tensorflow in creating an LSTM network.

6.1.5 Train the Model

Once the network is created, the next step is to train the network, the training is done with the imported and scaled trained data. The loss measure is Root Mean Square and the training is done till the loss is less than 1 percent. In order to get the best result, Parameter tuning is done as a result the best-trained network is obtained.

6.1.6 Import the Test Data

Once the training is done, the next step is to import the test data and the important thing to note is that the test data should be scaled to the similar values of the trained data. This should always be check. Once the scaled trained data is imported the trained model will be applied to this test data and the result is stored in a variable

6.1.7 Visualize the Result

Once the predicted data is obtained, it is visualized. In this process, both the test value and the predicted values are plotted in a scatter graph and the result a visualized.

6.1.8 Calculate the Efficiency

When all the steps are over, the final step is to calculate the efficiency of the model. This calculation will tell us how reliable the trained model is and how much it can be depended. The lower the loss the better the efficiency of the trained model.

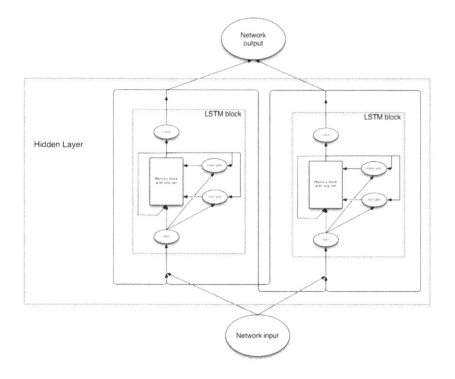

Fig[6.2]: LSTM Architectural Diagram

There are several architectures of LSTM units. A common architecture is composed of a memory cell, an input gate, an output gate and a forget gate.

An LSTM (memory) cell stores a value (or state), for either long or short time periods. This is achieved by using an identity (or no) activation function for the memory cell. In this way, when an LSTM network (that is an RNN composed of LSTM units) is trained with backpropagation through time, the gradient does not tend to vanish.

The LSTM gates compute an activation, often using the logistic function. Intuitively, the input gate controls the extent to which a new value flows into the cell, the forget gate controls the extent to which a value remains in the cell and the output gate controls the extent to which the value in the cell is used to compute the output activation of the LSTM unit.

There are connections into and out of these gates. A few connections are recurrent. The weights of these connections, which need to be learned during training, of an LSTM unit are used to direct the operation of the gates. Each of the gates has its own parameters, which is weights and biases, from other possible units outside the LSTM unit.

CHAPTER 7

SYSTEM REQUIREMENT

- **PROCESSOR**

    Intel Core i5 or Intel Core i7

- **RAM**

    8 GB or above

- **CPU SPEED**

    2.5 GHz or above

- **GPU**

    NVIDIA GTX1080

- **OPERATING SYSTEM**

    Windows 10

- **STORAGE**

    500 GB or above

- **COMPILER**

    Anaconda Python 3.5 with Spyder Compiler

CHAPTER 8

IMPLEMENTATION

8.1 DATA PREPROCESSING

8.1.1 Libraries Import

The First library that we will be importing is the Pandas library. As discussed before Pandas is an open source library providing high-performance, easy-to-use data structures and data analysis tools for the Python programming language. The main advantage of this library is that is allowed to import any datafile like CSV or Excel file with just a line of code.

The second library that we will be importing is the Numpy library. As discussed is the fundamental package for scientific computing with Python. It contains among other things, a powerful N-dimensional array objects sophisticated (broadcasting) functions. Besides its obvious scientific uses, NumPy can also be used as an efficient multi-dimensional container of generic data. Since we will be importing a larger amount of dataset it is preferable to use Numpy for array manipulations.

The Third Library that we will be importing is the Matplotlib library. Matplotlib is a Python 2D plotting library which produces publication quality figures in a variety of hardcopy formats and interactive environments across platforms. Matplotlib tries to make easy things easy and hard things possible. You can generate plots, histograms, power spectra, bar charts, error charts, scatterplots, etc., with just a few lines of code. Since we will visualize the data it is preferable to you this library.

The Fourth Library that we will be importing is the Scikit-learn. As discussed earlier Scikit-learn is a free software machine learning library for the Python programming language. The main reason of this library is that we will be using the MinMaxScaler from this library which will be used to scale the values to a specific range in order to get great results.

```
import pandas as pd
import numpy as np
import matplotlib.pyplot as plt
from sklearn.preprocessing import MinMaxScaler
```

Compilation

```
IPython 6.1.0 -- An enhanced Interactive Python.

In [1]: import pandas as pd
   ...: import numpy as np
   ...: import matplotlib.pyplot as plt
   ...: from sklearn.preprocessing import MinMaxScaler

In [2]:
```

8.1.2 Importing the Training Set

The next step is to import the dataset which we have collected. This dataset has been stored in a .csv file so we will use the panda's library to import the dataset. Once the dataset has been imported the next part is to split the dataset into the training set of data's in which the neural network will be trained. The import part of the dataset statements and the splitting the training data are as follows:

Dataset and Training set

```
dataset = pd.read_csv('stock.csv')
train_set = dataset.iloc[:, 1:2].values
```

Compilation

```
In [2]: dataset = pd.read_csv('stock.csv')
   ...: train_set = dataset.iloc[:, 1:2].values

In [3]:
```

Index	Date	Open	High	Low	Close	Volume
0	1/3/2012	325.25	332.83	324.97	663.59	7,380,500
1	1/4/2012	331.27	333.87	329.08	666.45	5,749,400
2	1/5/2012	329.83	330.75	326.89	657.21	6,590,300
3	1/6/2012	328.34	328.77	323.68	648.24	5,405,900
4	1/9/2012	322.04	322.29	309.46	620.76	11,688,800
5	1/10/2012	313.7	315.72	307.3	621.43	8,824,000
6	1/11/2012	310.59	313.52	309.4	624.25	4,817,800
7	1/12/2012	314.43	315.26	312.08	627.92	3,764,400
8	1/13/2012	311.96	312.3	309.37	623.28	4,631,800
9	1/17/2012	314.81	314.81	311.67	626.86	3,832,800
10	1/18/2012	312.14	315.82	309.9	631.18	5,544,000
11	1/19/2012	319.3	319.3	314.55	637.82	12,657,800
12	1/20/2012	294.16	294.4	289.76	584.39	21,231,800
13	1/23/2012	291.91	293.23	290.49	583.92	6,851,300
14	1/24/2012	292.07	292.74	287.92	579.34	6,134,400
15	1/25/2012	287.68	288.27	282.13	567.93	10,012,700

Fig[8.1]: Dataset Dataframe

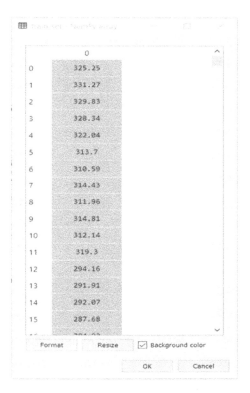

Fig[8.2]: Training set Dataframe

8.1.3 Feature Scaling

Once the dataset has been split into the training set, the next step is to apply the Scaling features to the set. The MinMaxScaler will be used for this problem. This scaling feature are applied to the training set and when it is applied all the values are scaled between the ranges 0 – 1 as we specify that the value has to be between that range

Scaling feature

```
scaler = MinMaxScaler(feature_range = (0, 1))
train_set_scaled = scaler.fit_transform(train_set)
```

```
In [3]: scaler = MinMaxScaler(feature_range = (0, 1))
   ...: train_set_scaled = scaler.fit_transform(train_set)

In [4]:
```

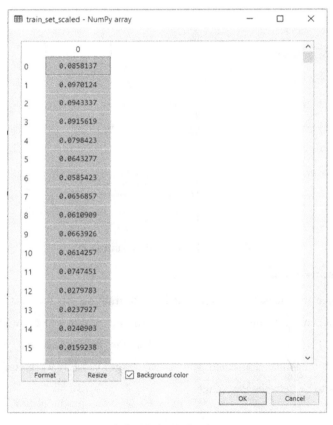

Fig[8.3]: Scaled values

8.1.4 Inputs and Outputs

Once the training set has been scaled the next step is to split the set into the Dependent set and the Independent set. In this, we will be using Xtrain and Ytrain as our variable name for the independent set and dependent set.

X train and Y train

```
Xtrain = train_set_scaled[0:1257]
Ytrain = train_set_scaled[1:1258]
```

Compilation

```
In [6]: Xtrain = train_set_scaled[0:1257]
   ...: Ytrain = train_set_scaled[1:1258]

In [7]:
```

Fig[8.4]: X train and Y train Dataframe

8.1.5 Reshaping

The next step is to reshape the Xtrain array from 2 dimensions to 3 dimensions. This is because the 2 dimensions have 2 features which are the size and the features array, but we need 3 dimensions because it has to include the previous 2 dimensions and an additional dimension which is the timestamp. The other important thing to note is that the Keras always expects a 3-dimensional array. And so we are again using Numpy to do this.

Reshaping

```
Xtrain = np.reshape(Xtrain, (Xtrain.shape[0], Xtrain.shape[1], 1))
```

Compiling

```
In [7]: Xtrain = np.reshape(Xtrain, (Xtrain.shape[0], Xtrain.shape[1], 1))

In [8]:
```

2 Dimension to 3 Dimension

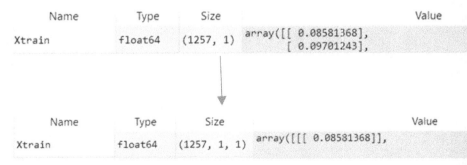

8.2 BUILDING THE RECURRENT NEURAL NETWORK (LSTM)

8.2.1 Libraries Import

The First library that I will be importing is the Keras library. This library is what we will be using to construct the LSTM Network.

The First thing that we will be importing from the Keras library, is that of the Sequential model. This actually tells that we will be using a sequential model in our neural network and not a Graph model.

The Second thing that we will be importing from the Keras library, is that of the Dense layers. This actually tells that we will be using a Dense layer in our neural network.

The Third thing that we will be importing from the Keras library, is that of the LSTM itself. This actually tells that we will be using an LSTM model in our neural network. This actually makes it easier for us to construct an LSTM network.

The Final thing that we will be importing from the Keras library, is that of the Dropout. This is mainly used to reduce the factor of overfitting in the neural network layer and giving an edge over our results.

Importing all the required Libraries

```
from keras.models import Sequential
from keras.layers import Dense
from keras.layers import LSTM
from keras.layers import Dropout
```

```
In [8]: from keras.models import Sequential
   ...: from keras.layers import Dense
   ...: from keras.layers import LSTM
   ...: from keras.layers import Dropout
Using TensorFlow backend.

In [9]:
```

It can be seen that once the libraries are imported and compiler, it says that "USING TENSORFLOW BACKEND", this is because Keras uses TensorFlow at the backed for the construction of the Neural network. In other words, Keras is built over TensorFlow, and Keras will act as an API for TensorFlow.

8.2.2 LSTM Construction

The first step in constructing the LSTM network is to create an object for the Sequential class that we imported from the Keras library. This is where we will be specifying that we will be using the sequential model.

```
model = Sequential()
```

The next step is to create the LSTM layer itself. This is done with the help of the LSTM class that was imported from the Keras library as well. When using this class there are some parameters that have to be passed on to this class, which defines the structure of the LSTM network. The most important parameters that have to be passed or the input dimension, output dimensions, activation function.

Another thing to note in creating the LSTM network is that, when multiple layers are created, only the first layer need the input dimension, whereas the other layer does not require the input dimension but is very important that the output dimension is specified in each layer.

```
model.add(LSTM(units = 4, return_sequences = True,
               activation = 'sigmoid', input_shape = (None, 1)))
```

In case of multiple layers, the may arise a problem called the problem of OverFitting. In order to avoid this problem, Keras provides a class called the Dropout, which can be imported from the Keras Library itself. This class when used avoid the problem of overfitting and help to give an edge over our result.

```
model.add(LSTM(units = 50, return_sequences = True))
model.add(Dropout(0.2))

model.add(LSTM(units = 50, return_sequences = True))
model.add(Dropout(0.2))
```

One the LSTM network is created, the next step is to create a Dense Layer. This layer is what it is used for the creation of the output layer. As similar to the previous case, the input dimensions need not be specified but it's compulsory that the output parameter is specified.

```
model.add(Dense(units = 1))
```

Once all these above steps are done the very next step is to create a connection between the layers. This is done with the help of a function called compile. This function takes in parameters and is very much important that u specify them. The parameters that have to be specified are Optimizer, Loss, and Accuracy.

```
model.compile(optimizer = 'adam', loss = 'mean_squared_error')
```

8.2.3 Model Fitting

This is the final step in building the Recurrent Neural Network. Once the model is compiled, the next step is to train the model with the training data. This step in training is called Model Fitting. There are some important parameters that have to be passed. Some of them are training data, a number of epochs and batch size.

```
model.fit(Xtrain, Ytrain, epochs = 200, batch_size = 32)
```

Compiling

```
In [3]: model.fit(Xtrain, Ytrain, epochs = 25, batch_size = 32)
Epoch 1/25
1257/1257 [==============================] - ETA: 2:22:50 - loss: 0.8233 - acc: 0.5463
```

8.3 PREDICTION

8.3.1 Importing the Test Data

The next step is to import the test dataset which we have collected. This dataset has been stored in the .csv file so we will use the panda's library to import the dataset. The import part of the dataset statements are as follows:

```
In [4]: test = pd.read_csv('Test.csv')
   ...: testX = test.iloc[:,1:2].values
```

Compiling

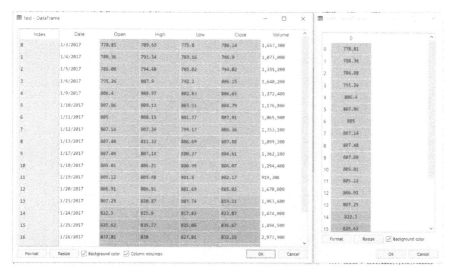

Fig[8.5]: Data Structure

8.3.2 Scaling and Reshaping Test Data

This scaling feature is applied to the test set and when it is applied all the values are scaled between the ranges 0 – 1.This is because previously the model has been trained on the scaled data of the training set and so its very important that the test data is also scaled to the same range with the same ratio. This is done with the help of the transform method.

The next step is to reshape from 2 dimensions to 3 dimensions. This is because the 2 dimensions have 2 features which are the size and the features array, but we need 3 dimensions because it has to include the previous 2 dimensions and an additional dimension which is the timestamp. The other important thing to note is that the Keras always expects a 3-dimensional array. And so we are again using Numpy to do this.

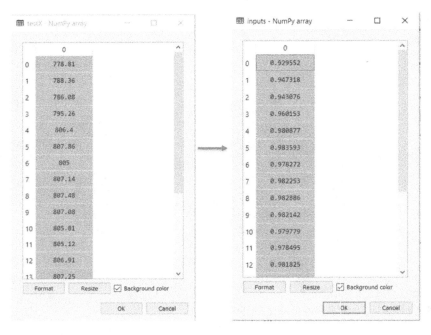

Fig[8.6]: Scaling

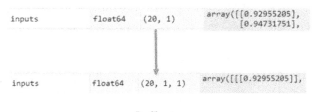

Re-Shaping

8.3.3 Predicting Test Data

Now, the Final step, predicting the result with the test data. The model is already trained and now the only step remaining is to predict the value of the test result. This is done with the help of the predict method. This method takes in the scaled values and predicts the result.

Another important thing to be noted is that the result which is obtained is a scaled value. So it has to be noted that the vales have to be scaled back. For this, inverse scaler method from the scaler object is used so that the obtained result will be reverse scaled to the original value.

```
predS = model.predict(inputs)
pred = scaler.inverse_transform(predS)
```

Predicting and Inverse Scaling

	0
0	0.924932
1	0.942109
2	0.938011
3	0.954502
4	0.974479
5	0.977094
6	0.97197
7	0.975804
8	0.976414
9	0.975697
10	0.973422
11	0.972186
12	0.975393
13	0.976002

Fig[8.7]: Prediction (Scaled)

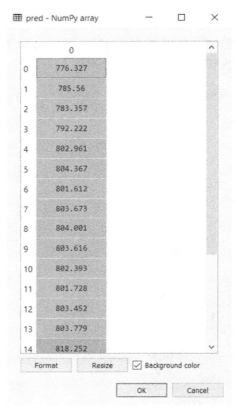

Fig[8.8]: Prediction (Reverse Scaled)

8.4 VISUALIZATION AND RESULTS

This is the final part. The Moment of Truth.

8.4.1 Visualization

As discussed before two libraries will be used for visualizing the result obtained from the model.

The first library is the mathplotlib library which will be used to visualize the result in the console and mostly used for debugging the problem that may arise when compiling. Also, the result can be visualized in the console it's not preferred.

```
plt.plot(testX,color = 'red',label='real price')
plt.plot(pred,color = 'blue',label='Predicted price')
plt.title('lalalalalal')
plt.xlabel('time')
plt.ylabel('Stock price')
plt.legend()
plt.show()
```

Using the Mathplotlib library

```
In [9]: plt.plot(testX,color = 'red',label='real price')
   ...: plt.plot(pred,color = 'blue',label='Predicted price')
   ...: plt.title('Prediction')
   ...: plt.xlabel('time')
   ...: plt.ylabel('Stock price')
   ...: plt.legend()
   ...: plt.show()
```

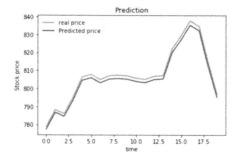

Fig[8.9]: Visualizing using the Mathplot library

So we will be using a library called Plotly, which we will be using to visualize the result in a much more clear way. The Main advantage of this library is that it's an offline library which gives you a much more detailed view of the result that is being visualized.

```python
import plotly.plotly as py
from plotly.graph_objs import Scatter, Figure, Layout
from plotly.offline import download_plotlyjs, init_notebook_mode, plot, iplot

trace1 = Scatter(
    x=xplot,
    y=yrplot,
    name = 'Real Stock Price',

)

trace2 = Scatter(
    x=xplot,
    y=ypplot,
    name = 'Predicted Stock Price'
)

plot({
    'data': [trace1,trace2],
    'layout': {
            'title': 'VISUAL RESULTS',
            'font': dict(size=16)
        }
    }
    )
```

VISUAL RESULTS

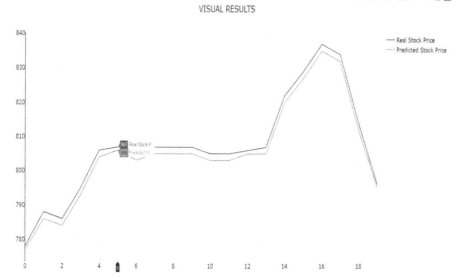

Fig[8.10]: Visualizing using the Plotly library

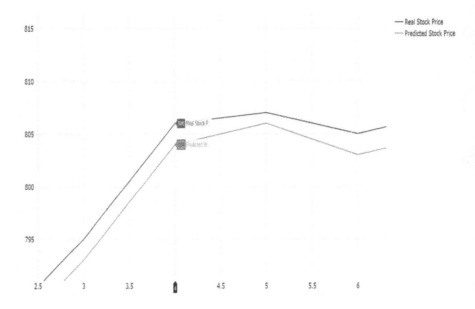

Fig[8.11]: Visualizing using the Plotly library (Zoomed in)

8.4.2 Results

For analyzing the efficiency of the system we are used the Root Mean Square Error(RMSE). The error or the difference between the target and the obtained output value is minimized by using RMSE value. RMSE is the square root of the mean/average of the square of all of the error. The use of RMSE is highly common and it makes an excellent general purpose error metric for numerical predictions. Compared to the similar Mean Absolute Error, RMSE amplifies and severely punishes large errors.

61

$$\mathrm{RMSE} = \sqrt{\sum \frac{(y_{pred} - y_{ref})^2}{N}}$$

RMSE Formula

```
error = math.sqrt(mean_squared_error(testX,pred))
error = error/(sum(testX)/testX.shape[0])
percent = error*100

print('-------------------------------------------------')
print ('RMSE:'+str(error))
print ('Percentage:'+str(percent[0])+' %')
print('-------------------------------------------------')
```

Fig [8.12]: RMSE Calculation Code

```
In [3]: from sklearn.metrics import mean_squared_error
   ...: import math
   ...:
   ...: error = math.sqrt(mean_squared_error(testX,pred))
   ...: error = error/(sum(testX)/testX.shape[0])
   ...: percent = error*100
   ...:
   ...: print('-------------------------------------------------')
   ...: print ('RMSE:'+str(error[0]))
   ...: print ('Percentage:'+str(percent[0])+' %')
   ...: print('-------------------------------------------------')
-------------------------------------------
RMSE:0.0023188896186739742
Percentage:0.23188896186739744 %
-------------------------------------------
```

Fig[8.13]: Compilation

CONCLUSION AND FUTURE WORK

The popularity of stock market trading is growing rapidly, which is encouraging researchers to find out new methods for the prediction using new techniques. The forecasting technique is not only helping the researchers but it also helps investors and any person dealing with the stock market. In order to help predict the stock indices, a forecasting model with good accuracy is required.

In this work, we have used one of the most precise forecasting technology using Recurrent Neural Network and Long Short-Term Memory unit which helps investors, analysts or any person interested in investing in the stock market by providing them a good knowledge of the future situation of the stock market.

In future, we would apply this model and take decisions in investing on stock markets based on the results of this model. We would also make this model as dynamic as possible by adding it as an additional feature.

PROJECT FLOW

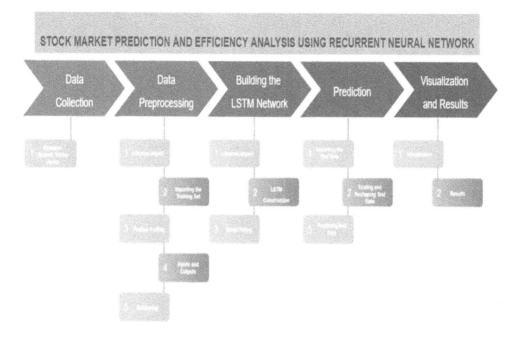

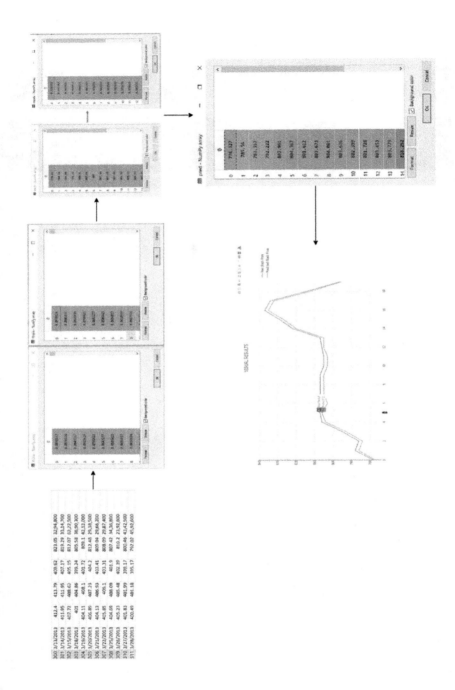

REFERENCES

[1]   Fazle Karim, Somshubra Majumdar, Houshang Darabi and Shun Chen "LSTM Fully Convolutional Networks for Time Series Classification" *September 2017 IEEE International Conference*

[2]   Chen Qian, Wenjie Zheng "Stock Market Trends Prediction after Earning Release" *2016 Stanford Publication*

[3]   Klaus Greff, Rupesh K. Srivastava, Jan Koutnʹık, Bas R. Steunebrink, Jurgen Schmidhuber "LSTM: A Search Space Odyssey" *March 2015 IEEE Transactions on Neural Networks and Learning Systems*

[4]   Andrej Karpathy, Justin Johnson, Li Fei-Fei "VISUALIZING AND UNDERSTANDING RECURRENT NETWORKS" *June 2015 Stanford Publication*

[5]   Stefan Lauren Dra. Harlili S., M.Sc "Stock Trend Prediction Using Simple Moving Average Supported by News Classification" *2014 International Conference of Advanced Informatics: Concept, Theory, and Application (ICAICTA).*

[6]   Razvan Pascanu, Tomas Mikolov, Yoshua Bengio "Difficulty of training recurrent neural networks" *February 2013 ICML'13 Proceedings of the 30th International Conference on International Conference on Machine Learning - Volume 28*

[7]   Xavier Glorot Antoine Bordes Yoshua Bengio "Deep Sparse Rectifier Neural Networks" *2011 in AISTATS*

[8]   Palacios Giner Alor-Hernandez, Ruben Posada-Gomez "Improving N Calculation of the RSI Financial Indicator Using Neural Networks" *2010 International Journal on Recent and Innovation Trends in Computing and Communication, Volume 18.*

[9]   Lamartine Almeida Teixeira Adriano Lorena Inácio de Oliveira "Predicting Stock Trends through Technical Analysis and Nearest Neighbor Classification" *February 2009 IEEE International Conference on Systems, Man, and Cybernetics Conference on Systems, Man, and Cybernetics*

[10]   Yoshua bengio, Patrice Simard and Paolo Frasconi "Learning Long term Dependencies with Gradient Descent is difficult" *March 1994 IEEE Transactions on Neural Networks and Learning Systems*

YOUR KNOWLEDGE HAS VALUE

- We will publish your bachelor's and master's thesis, essays and papers

- Your own eBook and book - sold worldwide in all relevant shops

- Earn money with each sale

Upload your text at www.GRIN.com and publish for free

www.ingramcontent.com/pod-product-compliance
Lightning Source LLC
La Vergne TN
LVHW042124070326
832902LV00036B/838